the Gienna Workshop

Pomegranate
SAN FRANCISCO

Pomegranate Communications, Inc.
Box 808022, Petaluma CA 94975
800 227 1428; www.pomegranate.com

Pomegranate Europe Ltd.
Unit 1, Heathcote Business Centre, Hurlbutt Road
Warwick, Warwickshire CV34 6TD, UK
[+44] 0 1926 430111; sales@pomeurope.co.uk

ISBN 978-0-7649-5053-7
Pomegranate Catalog No. AA596

Pomegranate publishes books of postcards on a wide range of subjects.
Please contact the publisher for more information.

Cover designed by Oky Sulistio
Printed in Korea

18 17 16 15 14 13 12 11 10 09   10 9 8 7 6 5 4 3 2 1

To facilitate detachment of the postcards from this book, fold each card along its perforation line before tearing.

Founded in 1903 by Josef Hoffmann (1870–1956) and Kolo Moser (1868–1918), the Vienna Workshop (Wiener Werkstätte) took as its philosophical model William Morris's Art Workers' Guild; like Morris's organization, the Vienna Workshop was anti-industrial and dedicated to the creativity of the individual artisan. As a bastion of modernism, the Vienna Workshop's activities often overlapped with those of the Secession (an artists' organization founded in 1898 by Gustav Klimt and his associates to exhibit the new art) and the Kunstgewerbeschule, a school in which the new principles were taught.

Over its thirty-year existence, the artists and designers of the Vienna Workshop worked in an almost unlimited number of fields, including glass, ceramics and china, theater design, fashion design, jewelry, typography, hand bookbinding, wallpapers, textiles, and architecture (the latter considered by some the field of its crowning achievement—the Stoclet Palace, designed by Josef Hoffman, 1905–1910).

In 1907 the Vienna Workshop, drawing upon an earlier idea of Hoffmann, Moser, and Olbrich, began to publish artists' postcards. Their purpose was to draw attention to the current activities of the Workshop, but as time went on the postcards seemed to become a design end in themselves. Between 1907 and 1914 the Workshop published over 1,000 numbered postcard editions. The selection of thirty postcards reproduced here includes designs by such celebrated artists as Hoffmann, Diveky, Schiele, Hoppe, and Jung.

5·10

Pomegranate, Box 808022, Petaluma, CA 94975

THE VIENNA WORKSHOP
Egon Schiele (Austrian, 1890–1918)
Number 290 in a series of postcards published by the
Wiener Werkstätte (Vienna Workshop), 1907–1914
From the collection of Der Salzburger Landessammlungen
Rupertinum, Austria

TÊTE A TÊTE AM WOLKENKRATZER 968. ETAGE

Pomegranate, Box 808022, Petaluma, CA 94975

THE VIENNA WORKSHOP

Moriz Jung (Czechoslovakian, 1885–1915)
Tête à Tête am Wolkenkratzer 968. Etage (Tête-à-tête at the Skyscraper, Apartment 968)
Number 340 in a series of postcards published by the
Wiener Werkstätte (Vienna Workshop), 1907–1914
From the collection of Der Salzburger Landessammlungen
Rupertinum, Austria

Pomegranate, Box 808022, Petaluma, CA 94975

THE VIENNA WORKSHOP
Mela Koehler (Austrian, 1887–1960)
Number 523 in a series of postcards published by the
Wiener Werkstätte (Vienna Workshop), 1907–1914
From the collection of Der Salzburger Landessammlungen
Rupertinum, Austria

ALTER·HOF·NEUSTIFTGASSE·

Pomegranate, Box 808022, Petaluma, CA 94975

THE VIENNA WORKSHOP

Emil Hoppe (Austrian, 1876–1957)
Alter Hof, Neustiftgasse (Old Courtyard, Neustift Street)
Number 47 in a series of postcards published by the
Wiener Werkstätte (Vienna Workshop), 1907–1914
From the collection of Der Salzburger Landessammlungen
Rupertinum, Austria

WIENER CAFE: DER LITTERAT.

Pomegranate, Box 808022, Petaluma, CA 94975

THE VIENNA WORKSHOP

Moriz Jung (Czechoslovakian, 1885–1915)
Wiener Cafe: Der Literat (*Vienna Cafe: The Writer*)
Number 532 in a series of postcards published by the
Wiener Werkstätte (Vienna Workshop), 1907–1914
From the collection of Der Salzburger Landessammlungen
Rupertinum, Austria

Pomegranate, Box 808022, Petaluma, CA 94975

THE VIENNA WORKSHOP
Egon Schiele (Austrian, 1890–1918)
Number 289 in a series of postcards published by the
Wiener Werkstätte (Vienna Workshop), 1907–1914
From the collection of Der Salzburger Landessammlungen
Rupertinum, Austria

THE VIENNA WORKSHOP

Artist unknown
Number 578 in a series of postcards published by the
Wiener Werkstätte (Vienna Workshop), 1907–1914
From the collection of Der Salzburger Landessammlungen
Rupertinum, Austria

Pomegranate, Box 808022, Petaluma, CA 94975

Pomegranate, Box 808022, Petaluma, CA 94975

THE VIENNA WORKSHOP
Artist unknown
Number 548 in a series of postcards published by the
Wiener Werkstätte (Vienna Workshop), 1907–1914
From the collection of Der Salzburger Landessammlungen
Rupertinum, Austria

Pomegranate, Box 808022, Petaluma, CA 94975

THE VIENNA WORKSHOP
Egon Schiele (Austrian, 1890–1918)
Number 288 in a series of postcards published by the
Wiener Werkstätte (Vienna Workshop), 1907–1914
From the collection of Der Salzburger Landessammlungen
Rupertinum, Austria

THE VIENNA WORKSHOP
Josef Diveky (Hungarian, 1887–1951)
Number 247 in a series of postcards published by the
Wiener Werkstätte (Vienna Workshop), 1907–1914
From the collection of Der Salzburger Landessammlungen
Rupertinum, Austria

Pomegranate, Box 808022, Petaluma, CA 94975

Pomegranate, Box 808022, Petaluma, CA 94975

THE VIENNA WORKSHOP
Rudolf Kalvach (Austrian, 1883–1932)
Number 29 in a series of postcards published by the
Wiener Werkstätte (Vienna Workshop), 1907–1914
From the collection of Der Salzburger Landessammlungen
Rupertinum, Austria

KIRCHE IN ERDBERG

Pomegranate, Box 808022, Petaluma, CA 94975

THE VIENNA WORKSHOP

Emil Hoppe (Austrian, 1876–1957)
Kirche in Erdberg (Cherry in Erdberg)
Number 23 in a series of postcards published by the
Wiener Werkstätte (Vienna Workshop), 1907–1914
From the collection of Der Salzburger Landessammlungen
Rupertinum, Austria

Pomegranate, Box 808022, Petaluma, CA 94975

THE VIENNA WORKSHOP
Rudolf Kalvach (Austrian, 1883–1932)
Number 148 in a series of postcards published by the
Wiener Werkstätte (Vienna Workshop), 1907–1914

NAECHTLICHES GESPRAECH

Pomegranate, Box 808022, Petaluma, CA 94975

THE VIENNA WORKSHOP

Attributed to Moriz Jung (Czechoslovakian, 1885–1915)
Naechtliches Gespraech (*Conversation at Night*)
Number 66 in a series of postcards published by the
Wiener Werkstätte (Vienna Workshop), 1907–1914
From the collection of Der Salzburger Landessammlungen
Rupertinum, Austria

DIE SIEGREICHEN

Pomegranate, Box 808022, Petaluma, CA 94975

THE VIENNA WORKSHOP
Rudolf Kalvach (Austrian, 1883–1932)
Die Siegreichen (*The Victorious*)
Number 100 in a series of postcards published by the
Wiener Werkstätte (Vienna Workshop), 1907–1914
From the collection of Der Salzburger Landessammlungen
Rupertinum, Austria

Pomegranate, Box 808022, Petaluma, CA 94975

THE VIENNA WORKSHOP

Artist unknown
Number 676 in a series of postcards published by the
Wiener Werkstätte (Vienna Workshop), 1907–1914
From the collection of Der Salzburger Landessammlungen
Rupertinum, Austria

Pomegranate, Box 808022, Petaluma, CA 94975

THE VIENNA WORKSHOP
Josef Hoffmann (Austrian, 1870–1956)
Number 5 in a series of postcards published by the
Wiener Werkstätte (Vienna Workshop), 1907–1914
From the collection of Der Salzburger Landessammlungen
Rupertinum, Austria

Pomegranate, Box 808022, Petaluma, CA 94975

THE VIENNA WORKSHOP

Attributed to Susi Singer (Austrian, 1891– c. 1965)
Number 733 in a series of postcards published by the
Wiener Werkstätte (Vienna Workshop), 1907–1914
From the collection of Der Salzburger Landessammlungen
Rupertinum, Austria

Pomegranate, Box 808022, Petaluma, CA 94975

THE VIENNA WORKSHOP
Maria Likarz-Strauss (Polish, 1893–1956)
Number 564 in a series of postcards published by the
Wiener Werkstätte (Vienna Workshop), 1907–1914
From the collection of Der Salzburger Landessammlungen
Rupertinum, Austria

LEDA MIT DEM SCHWAN

WIENER WERKSTÄTTE WIEN I. GRABEN 15. POSTKARTE NO. 107

Pomegranate, Box 808022, Petaluma, CA 94975

THE VIENNA WORKSHOP
Rudolf Kalvach (Austrian, 1883–1932)
Leda mit dem Schwan (Leda with the Swan)
Number 107 in a series of postcards published by the
Wiener Werkstätte (Vienna Workshop), 1907–1914
From the collection of Der Salzburger Landessammlungen
Rupertinum, Austria

Pomegranate, Box 808022, Petaluma, CA 94975

THE VIENNA WORKSHOP
Mela Koehler (Austrian, 1887–1960)
Number 477 in a series of postcards published by the
Wiener Werkstätte (Vienna Workshop), 1907–1914
From the collection of Der Salzburger Landessammlungen
Rupertinum, Austria

Pomegranate, Box 808022, Petaluma, CA 94975

THE VIENNA WORKSHOP

Artist unknown
Number 541 in a series of postcards published by the
Wiener Werkstätte (Vienna Workshop), 1907–1914
From the collection of Der Salzburger Landessammlungen
Rupertinum, Austria

Pomegranate, Box 808022, Petaluma, CA 94975

THE VIENNA WORKSHOP
Ludwig Heinrich Jungnickel (Austrian, 1881–1965)
Number 381 in a series of postcards published by the
Wiener Werkstätte (Vienna Workshop), 1907–1914
From the collection of Der Salzburger Landessammlungen
Rupertinum, Austria

Pomegranate, Box 808022, Petaluma, CA 94975

THE VIENNA WORKSHOP
Hans Kalmsteiner (1886– c. 1916)
Kasperltheater (Puppet Theater)
Number 382 in a series of postcards published by the
Wiener Werkstätte (Vienna Workshop), 1907–1914
From the collection of Der Salzburger Landessammlungen
Rupertinum, Austria

DIE BERÜHMTE VOGELMEUTE
DES HERZOGS VON GRAMATNEISS

Pomegranate, Box 808022, Petaluma, CA 94975

THE VIENNA WORKSHOP
Moriz Jung (Czechoslovakian, 1885–1915)
Die Berühmte Vogelmeute des Herzogs von Gramatneiss
(The Famous Birdhounds of the Duke of Gramatneiss)
Number 344 in a series of postcards published by the
Wiener Werkstätte (Vienna Workshop), 1907–1914
From the collection of Der Salzburger Landessammlungen
Rupertinum, Austria

THE VIENNA WORKSHOP
Carl Krenek (Austrian, 1880–1948)
Number 253 in a series of postcards published by the
Wiener Werkstätte (Vienna Workshop), 1907–1914
From the collection of Der Salzburger Landessammlungen
Rupertinum, Austria

Pomegranate, Box 808022, Petaluma, CA 94975

Pomegranate, Box 808022, Petaluma, CA 94975

Pomegranate, Box 808022, Petaluma, CA 94975

THE VIENNA WORKSHOP
Rudolf Kalvach (Austrian, 1883–1932)
Number 94 in a series of postcards published by the
Wiener Werkstätte (Vienna Workshop), 1907–1914
From the collection of Der Salzburger Landessammlungen
Rupertinum, Austria

DER·WUNDERVOGEL·

THE VIENNA WORKSHOP
Josef Diveky (Hungarian, 1887–1951)
Der-Wundervogel (*The Miraculous Bird*)
Number 501 in a series of postcards published by the
Wiener Werkstätte (Vienna Workshop), 1907–1914
From the collection of Der Salzburger Landessammlungen
Rupertinum, Austria

Pomegranate, Box 808022, Petaluma, CA 94975

Pomegranate, Box 808022, Petaluma, CA 94975

THE VIENNA WORKSHOP
Maria Likarz-Strauss (Polish, 1893–1956)
Number 557 in a series of postcards published by the
Wiener Werkstätte (Vienna Workshop), 1907–1914
From the collection of Der Salzburger Landessammlungen
Rupertinum, Austria